Underwater

A FIRST-HAND ACCOUNT

# Fish Tricks

Written by Elizabeth Cook

Photography by Robert Yin

HAMERAY

PUBLISHING GROUP

Published in the United States of America
by the Hameray Publishing Group, Inc.


Text © Elizabeth Cook
Published 2009


Publisher: Christine Yuen
Editorial Consultant: Adria Klein
Editor: Sara Sarver
Designer: Lois Stanfield

Photo credits: Robert Yin
The photo of the group of whitetip reef sharks on page 24 and the shark on
page 25 are courtesy of Elizabeth Cook

ISBN 978-1-60559-100-1

Printed in China

1 2 3 4 5 SIP 13 12 11 10 9

# Contents

## CHAPTER 1

# Fish Watching

Fish have some pretty neat tricks. Some live in odd places. Some do tricky things with eggs. And some really tricky fish ride on other ocean animals.

Marine biologists are scientists who watch ocean animals. They spend many hours studying fish. They have learned just how tricky fish can be.

They learned that fish sleep with their eyes open. They know that some fish hold their eggs in their mouths. And they found out that male sea horses have babies—now that's quite a trick!

◀ Marine biologists study fish and animals in the ocean.

## CHAPTER 2

# Finding a Home

Ocean animals make their homes in different places. Some live in the open ocean. Some prefer the safety of the cracks and **crevices** of the reef. Others, like the octopus, have an interesting trick. They make a home in things they find on the ocean floor. If they find a bottle or a can, they may move right in. After all, a bottle or a can is a safe place from **predators** such as sharks.

Many ocean animals also perform special tricks under the sand. Some hide there for safety. Others hide there waiting for dinner to pass by. And some fish dig out a **burrow** to live in under the sand.

◀ An octopus has made its home in an old jar.

▲ A female octopus hides with her eggs inside two pieces of a coconut shell.

## Hiding in a Coconut Shell

The octopus is a clever and tricky animal. Sometimes it finds a strange object like a can or a bottle on the ocean floor. Using an arm, it will reach out and touch it. It may wonder if the object would make a nice home.

Old coconut shells can be a good home for some octopuses. The female octopus likes to nest in these shells. Hidden inside, she can safely wait with her eggs until they **hatch**. The male octopus uses coconut shells as a hideout. Once inside, he waits for a good meal to pass by.

**Cans, Bottles, and Old Tires**

Lots of small fish make homes out of things they find on the ocean floor. They settle into cans, bottles, and even old tires. Objects with narrow openings seem to be favorite places to hide. Narrow openings help keep hungry hunters from squeezing inside.

The moray eel is a long, **slithery** animal. Its special trick is fitting itself into oddly shaped spaces. An old tire is a good shape for an eel's home. It **coils** itself neatly inside the tire.

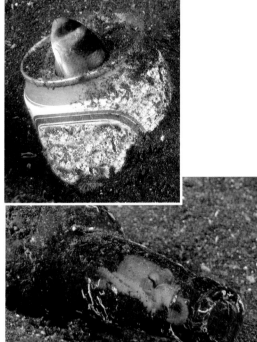

▲ Ocean animals can be very tricky—they use old bottles, cans, and tires as places to hide.

▲ Snake eels hide most of their body under the sand while waiting for dinner to pass by.

## A Tricky Hunter

The snake eel is a long, thin, snake-like animal. It spends a lot of time under the sand. It uses the hard tip at the end of its tail as a drill. It uses its tail to dig down into the sand. As it drills, it slides backward into the hole. When far enough under the sand, it stops.

The snake eel has a tricky way of hunting. With its body in its hole, it rests with its eyes and nose just above the sand. When a small animal swims by, the snake eel darts out of its hole and snaps up the prey.

This spotted garden eel is covered in small black spots. It also has three larger spots— one near its head, one near its middle, and one near its tail. ▶

## A Garden of Eels

The garden eel is another snake-like animal. Hundreds of garden eels live in a **colony** in the ocean floor.

The garden eel's skin produces a clear, sticky liquid. This liquid is called mucus. As the eel wiggles tail-first into the hole, the mucus glues the grains of sand together. The glued sand keeps the walls from caving in. That is pretty tricky.

When garden eels feed, they rise up from their burrows and catch tiny animals and fish eggs that float by. But they always keep their tails just inside the burrows.

The garden eels' best trick is their disappearing act. When scared, they quickly back tail-first into their burrows. One second they are all above the sand; the next second the sandy ocean floor looks empty. They stay in their burrows until all danger has passed. Then, carefully, they poke their heads out of the sand to see if it is safe to come out.

## Under the Sand

The jawfish is a fish that has a big, wide mouth and a thick body. It is a master at building a home under the ocean's sandy floor. When digging a tunnel under the sand, the jawfish uses its mouth in a tricky way. It scoops up mouthfuls of sand. Then it spits the sand out of the tunnel.

During the day, the jawfish stays just outside the entry to its home. When afraid, it slides backward or dives head-first into its burrow. To keep safe at night, some jawfish have a special trick. They push a rock across the opening to the burrow to keep predators out.

▲ A jawfish at the entrance to its burrow.

▲ The snapping shrimp waits next to its fish friend, the shrimp goby.

The snapping shrimp does not see very well. It is often called a blind shrimp. But it has a clever trick. It shares its home with a fish. And it uses that fish to warn itself of danger.

First, the snapping shrimp uses its large front claws to dig a deep burrow. When the burrow is ready, a small fish called a shrimp goby moves in. Both the shrimp and the goby like to spend time just outside the hole of the burrow. But the shrimp cannot see predators very well. So it uses its special trick. It keeps one of its feelers touching the goby.

When danger approaches, the goby flicks its tail. The shrimp's feeler feels the goby's warning tail flick. The shrimp quickly dashes inside the burrow. If the goby is scared too, it leaps into the burrow as well.

The snapping shrimp has another trick. Its especially large claw can make a loud cracking noise underwater. The "snap" is so loud that it can knock out or stun an enemy.

Mantis Shrimp with Eggs

# CHAPTER 3

# Clever Tricks with Eggs

Several types of fish, as well as some other ocean animals, play clever tricks with their eggs. Some fish hold their eggs in their mouths while waiting for them to hatch. Some ocean animals try to trick predators who like to eat their eggs. They hide their eggs in sneaky places, one egg at a time. And the large, colorful mantis shrimp has a very cute trick—she carries her eggs with her front legs.

◀ Mantis shrimp lay many hundreds of eggs.

## Big, Wide Mouths

The jawfish and the cardinalfish have big, wide mouths. Their mouths are well suited for a special trick. The female of each **species** produces a ball of eggs. The male produces special **cells** called sperm cells. Once the sperm cells join the eggs, the eggs can grow into baby fish. This process is called fertilization.

Eggs

▲ The jawfish with eggs in its mouth.

Eggs

▲  The male cardinalfish carries eggs in its mouth.

Here's the tricky part. Once the eggs are fertilized, the male sucks the eggs into his mouth. Then he gently holds them there. Once in a while, he spits the eggs out. Then he quickly sucks them back in. This cleans the eggs and provides them with extra **oxygen**. With a mouth full of eggs, the male jawfish or cardinalfish cannot eat. He usually will not eat until the babies hatch from the eggs.

After the eggs hatch, one type of cardinalfish will let the baby fish live in its mouth for a few days. Other types of cardinalfish will eat the babies if they do not find a new home.

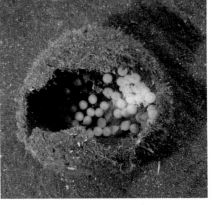

▲ A female flamboyant cuttlefish has hidden her eggs in the coconut shell.

◄ The flamboyant cuttlefish prefers to walk rather than swim.

## A Tricky Cuttlefish

There is a special animal called the flamboyant cuttlefish. This cuttlefish is called "flamboyant" because of the waves or "flames" of color that flow over its body. When excited, it flashes yellow, red, and black patterns across its skin. This small cuttlefish is a soft-bodied animal that is little enough to fit in a person's hand. It has eight arms and two **tentacles**.

The female flamboyant cuttlefish hides her eggs in a tricky way. She carefully lays her eggs one at a time. She hides them in cracks and under ledges on the coral reef. At times, she even hides them in empty coconut shells. Once the flamboyant cuttlefish hides her eggs, her job is done. When they are ready, the babies hatch from their eggs. They soon go hunting for their first meal.

# A FIRST-HAND ACCOUNT

On a late afternoon dive, I watched as a female mantis shrimp came out of her burrow. Her front legs were filled with a ball of tiny eggs. I held quite still, hoping not to disturb the shrimp. As I watched, the shrimp cleaned and turned the eggs. What a job she had! There were probably a thousand eggs. The mantis shrimp seemed very proud of all the eggs. When the cleaning was over, she carried her eggs back to the burrow.

▲ The peacock mantis shrimp carries her eggs with her front legs.

## CHAPTER 4

# Bedtime Tricks

Since fish do not have eyelids, do they sleep? That depends on what is meant by the word "sleep." Scientists do not think that fish sleep like people do. But they do know that fish rest.

Sometimes fish rest in a crack or a crevice. They may even tuck themselves under a ledge. Some ocean animals, such as stingrays, bury themselves under the sand. Once hidden, they will lay there quietly for long periods of time.

◄ Stingrays often bury themselves in sand when they get ready for a nap.

▲ Up on a ledge and on an old piece of wood, these parrotfish find a safe place to rest.

Like most people, many fish are awake during the day. Then they sleep at night. Scientists say these fish are diurnal. Fish that are active at night and sleep during the day are said to be nocturnal.

Nocturnal fish usually have special tools to help them hunt. They may have a very good sense of smell or hearing that they use while hunting in the dark.

## A Special Bubble

The parrotfish performs an interesting trick at bedtime. When a parrotfish is ready to sleep, it finds a snug spot on the reef. Then it blows a clear bubble around itself. The bubble is made of mucus. The parrotfish's mucus is a clear, slick liquid much like spit. The bubble covers the parrotfish. The bubble may keep hungry eels from smelling the fish and finding it. An eel would enjoy a parrotfish dinner. Inside the **cocoon**, the parrotfish can rest safely.

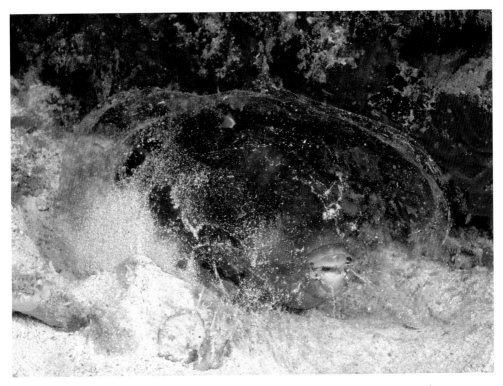

▲ Parrotfish have a most unusual trick—they sometimes sleep in a bubble.

◀ Like other sharks, whitetip reef sharks rest with their eyes wide open.

## Shark Eyes

The tricky thing about sharks is that scientists do not know if sharks sleep. They cannot tell because sharks' eyes are always open. Although sharks have eyelids, their eyelids do not move. They do not open and close the way people's eyelids do.

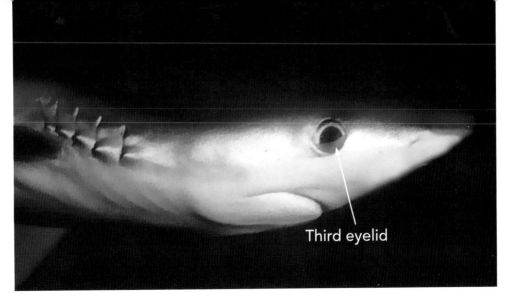

Third eyelid

▲ Some sharks have a special "third" eyelid.

The whitetip reef shark and the blue shark have a third eyelid on each eye. This special eyelid is called a nictating membrane.

The nictating membrane quickly rolls up over the eye when the shark bites at prey. The nictating membrane protects the eye from being hurt by the prey. The membrane covers the eye only during the attack. It does not cover the eye when the shark rests.

Some sharks, like the great white shark, have no third eyelid to protect their eyes. But they have an interesting trick. They roll their eyes up into their eye **sockets** when attacking prey. This way, their eyes are kept safe from biting fish or animals.

## CHAPTER 5

# Mr. Mom

How's this for tricky? Male sea horses get to be **pregnant**, not the females. But first, the male must capture the interest of a female sea horse. To attract a female, males compete with each other. Boxing is one of their favorite sports. First, they lower their heads. Then they use their snouts to try and punch their **rival**. A well-placed punch can push a rival four inches away.

◀ A pregnant pygmy sea horse on coral branches—this little sea horse is the size of a fingernail. The bumps on the snout and body match those of the coral it lives on.

▲ Sea horses blend in well with the sandy floor of the ocean and the plants around them.

Male sea horses also tail wrestle with each other. They wrap their tails around each other and push and pull. When one gives up, the game is over. The female may be **impressed** with the winner and accept it as a mate.

The number of sea horses in the world is growing smaller. Sea horses are often captured and dried. These are sold as **trinkets**. They are also used in Asian medicine. Live sea horses can be found in some pet stores. The number of sea horses captured for these purposes hurts their chance to survive as a species.

Sea horse couples perform a morning greeting. They dance for each other and change color. The female carries eggs inside her body. When the eggs are ready to be fertilized, the female places the eggs in the male's **pouch**. While the eggs are in his pouch, the male fertilizes them. The pouch gets larger as the eggs grow. It takes at least ten days for the babies to mature. When ready, the babies burst out of the pouch. Anywhere from ten to one hundred and fifty baby sea horses are born.

▲ Both sea horses and their relative the pipefish are dried and may be bought in Asian markets.

Banded Cleaner Shrimp

## CHAPTER 6

# Cleaning Stations

Fish often take part in a neat underwater trick. They visit a cleaning station to get their teeth cleaned. A cleaning station is a place where cleaner shrimp and cleaner fish gather. There they have an unusual job. Their job is to clean the teeth of fish, eels, and other ocean animals. They pick old food off the teeth of these animals.

Eels love to have their teeth cleaned. They slither close to the cleaner shrimp. Then they open their jaws wide. In a **trance**, they let the shrimp pick their teeth clean.

◀ Eels are favorite guests at the cleaner shrimp's cleaning station.

Fish also come to the cleaning station to have their teeth and skin cleaned. They wait in line, one after another. They yawn and open their **gills** wide. This invites the cleaner fish and shrimp to hop on board and start to work. The cleaner shrimp and fish pick the fish's teeth and gills clean. Then they work on the fish's scales.

▲ Fish hold very still while their skin and teeth are cleaned by cleaner fish and cleaner shrimp.

# A FIRST-HAND ACCOUNT

*On a recent dive, I watched the shrimp clean the fish's mouth and gills. Then I carefully drew near and put out my hand. Imagine my surprise when the shrimp came to work on me! Their tiny claws tickled my fingers.*

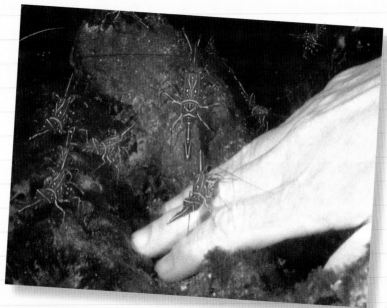

▲ Cleaner shrimp are willing to clean fish, both large and small, and even my fingers.

What's odd is that these cleaner fish and shrimp would normally be eaten by the fish that they clean. Instead, the fish being cleaned hold very still for their cleaning. They even let the cleaners nip around their eyes and **nostrils**.

## CHAPTER 7

# A Free Ride

Catching a free ride is a very useful trick. It is a trick some types of crabs, shrimp, and fish like to do. These crabs, shrimp, and fish pick out an animal. Then they hop on board. Wherever their ride goes, they go, too.

Some crabs, shrimp, and fish pick a slow ride. They might choose a sea urchin, which moves slowly, like a snail. Others pick a much faster ride. A speedy shark may be more to their liking.

◀ Two fish get a free ride on the belly of this sea turtle.

Zebra Crab

▲  The zebra crab catches a ride on an urchin.

## Hooking a Ride

The zebra crab is a small brown and white striped crab. It is often found riding on a fire urchin. The fire urchin is a round animal with many long, sharp spines. The little crab makes its home between the spines. The crab has a special trick it uses to hang on to the urchin. On the end of the crab's leg is a tiny hook. It uses its hook to hold on to the urchin's spines. The spines help keep the tiny zebra crab's home safe from predators.

## Riding on a Flower

The anemone shrimp also enjoys a free ride. This tiny shrimp makes its home on an anemone. An anemone is a soft, flowery-looking ocean animal. Anemones have many finger-like tentacles. Their tentacles sting fish that come too close. But for some reason, the anemone shrimp is not hurt by the sting. Instead, it hides between the tentacles. The sting of the tentacles keeps the shrimp safe from hungry fish.

▲ The see-through body of this little shrimp helps it hide on this flower-like animal.

▲ Since their "sucker" is on top of their head, these suckerfish are riding upside down on this sea turtle.

## A Speedy Ride

The suckerfish may be the biggest fish in the ocean to get a free ride. The suckerfish is a long, slender fish. It grows to nearly three feet long. It has a really odd trick.

The suckerfish has a round sucking plate on top of its head. The sucking plate is a muscle that acts like a pair of lips. The fish moves this muscle to make a sucking motion and stick itself to a larger fish.

When ready to go for a ride, the suckerfish swims near the fish it wants to ride on. It flattens and sticks the special sucking plate against the fish's body. It then gets a free ride and goes wherever the fish swims. When it wants to swim away it relaxes the muscle and slips off its ride.

▲ Sharks are not known to eat suckerfish—indeed, small suckerfish are sometimes found hiding in the mouths of sharks.

The suckerfish catches a ride this way with many ocean animals. Most often it attaches itself to turtles, sharks, or manta rays. The animals do not seem to be bothered by their guest. In fact, the suckerfish does them a favor. While riding with them, the suckerfish cleans **parasites** and dead skin off their bodies.

Suckerfish go by several names. They are also known as remoras, shark suckers, and whale suckers.

## CHAPTER 8

# Blowing Bubbles

Young sea lions are playful animals. The young ones find scuba divers very amusing. They dart around scuba divers, twisting and turning. They seem to be inviting the divers to play. They can swim a circle around a diver faster than the diver can turn his or her head.

The adult male protects his area or territory. His territory includes his harem. A sea lion harem is a group of adult and young female sea lions. It may also include very young pups.

◀ Young sea lions love to play.

▲  Young sea lions often blow bubbles through their noses when they play.

If the adult male wants a scuba diver to leave his territory, he has an interesting trick. He swims right up to the diver. Then he blows a stream of bubbles out his nose. Bubble blowing is a clear demand to the diver to leave. If the diver stays, the sea lion swims like a rocket through the water. He swims straight at the diver while blowing bubbles out his nose. If that doesn't scare the diver, the sea lion may try to nip or bite the diver with his sharp teeth.

# A FIRST-HAND ACCOUNT

*I lay on the bottom of the ocean while I watched the young sea lion pup. It came nose to nose with me. Then it swam happy circles around me. Its mother came and joined in the fun. They zoomed high and low in the ocean. Finally, the father sea lion came looking for them. As the father swam by, he blew bubbles in my face. He was asking me to leave. His family followed behind as he zoomed off into the blue water.*

◄ When I lay on the sand, the young sea lion did the same.

Then its father asked me to leave. ▶

# Protecting Our Blue Planet

## Ways We Can Help

- Continue to read about the ocean and the animals in it. Learning about the ocean helps people take better care of it.

- Learn about careers related to fish, aquariums, and marine biology by visiting the library. Read about different careers on the Science Careers page of the Monterey Bay Aquarium's Web site at: http://www.montereybayaquarium.org/lc/kids_place/kidseq_careers.asp.

- After visiting the library or the Web site above, write a short report about jobs related to fish. Then present it to a class or group to help them learn.

- Pick an animal to read about on the Explorer's Guide page of the Shedd Aquarium's Web site at: http://www.sheddaquarium.org/SEA/guide_eng.cfm?cat_id=1.

- Click on the animal's name and read about its diet and how it reproduces.

- Never buy trinkets made from dead ocean animals. Buying these items encourages people who sell them to continue killing the animals.

◀ Lots of fish mean this coral reef is very healthy.

# Fun Facts

## Does the garden eel stay in one home all its life?

The garden eel likes to stay in its home all its life. However, if its burrow is torn apart, it must make a new one. Animals like stingrays feed on the bottom of the ocean. They push the sand around looking for small crabs and things to eat. If they push a garden eel out of its burrow, the eel has to move and make a new home.

## Does the jawfish eat when it has its eggs in its mouth?

No, the jawfish does not eat while it has eggs in its mouth. Scientists believe that the jawfish does not eat at all during the time it is caring for the eggs. The jawfish spits the eggs out once in a while to clean them. But it does this very quickly. If a small meal floats by while the eggs are out, the jawfish might snap it up. But the male jawfish is most concerned with the safety of its eggs.

## How long does a parrotfish stay in its cocoon?

The parrotfish sleeps in its cocoon for only one night. And no one knows why, but the parrotfish does not make a cocoon each night.

## If animals use trash to make their home, why shouldn't people throw trash in the ocean?

Animals use empty bottles and old cans for safety. So why not throw trash in the ocean? One good reason is because scientists do not know enough about what happens to trash that ends up in the ocean. They do know that things like plastic bags choke and kill ocean animals that eat them. It's better not to use the ocean as a trash can but to keep it as clean as possible.

## What is the difference between a sea lion and a seal?

The sea lion has small ear flaps. The seal has none. The sea lion's back flippers can flip forward. This helps it walk forward. The seal is not able to walk with its rear flippers.

# Glossary

| | |
|---|---|
| **burrow** | A hole in the ground that an animal lives in |
| **cells** | Smallest parts of a person's body that are alive; skin is made up of millions of skin cells |
| **cocoon** | A covering that protects the creature inside it |
| **coils** | Twists into a circle |
| **colony** | A group of animals of the same kind that live near each other |
| **crevices** | Narrow openings |
| **gills** | Openings on each side of a fish's head that they use to breathe |
| **hatch** | To break out of an egg |
| **impressed** | Pleased with another person's or animal's skills or actions |
| **nostrils** | Holes in the nose through which animals breathe |
| **oxygen** | A gas that is part of the air that people and animals breathe |
| **parasites** | Tiny animals that live and feed on or in larger animals |
| **pouch** | A pocket some animals have for carrying eggs or young |
| **predators** | Animals that hunt other animals for food |
| **pregnant** | Having an unborn baby in the body |
| **rival** | An enemy |
| **slithery** | Sliding and snake-like |
| **sockets** | Openings in the head that hold the eyes |
| **species** | A group of plants or animals that mate and produce babies |
| **tentacles** | Long, finger-like body parts around the mouths of anemones and cuttlefish |
| **trance** | A state of dream-like calm |
| **trinkets** | Small toys or objects without much value |

# Index